The Art of Good Zzz's

Circadian Alignment, Relaxation, and Curing Insomnia Through Healthy Bedtime Routines

Dr. Melinda Hope

Table of Contents

Introduction

Are you tired of being tired? Do you find yourself tossing and turning, night after night, desperately seeking the elusive embrace of a peaceful slumber? If so, know this – you are not alone. We've all been there, caught in the relentless grip of insomnia, yearning for the sweet release of rest that seems to dance just out of reach.

I get it. I've been there, too.

In the quiet moments of the night, when the world sleeps, anxiety often takes center stage. The worries of the day and the uncertainties of tomorrow converge, casting a shadow over the stillness we so desperately crave. The frustration of sleepless nights becomes a heavy burden that colors our days, leaving us weary, irritable, and, let's face it, a bit desperate for a solution.

But, dear reader, there is hope.

Welcome to "The Art of Good Zzz's." In these pages, we embark on a journey together, a journey through the winding paths of circadian rhythms, the soothing landscapes of relaxation techniques, and the transformative power of healthy bedtime routines. This is not just a book; it's a companion, a guide, and a promise.

I understand the ache of insomnia, the weariness that seeps into your bones, and the yearning for the serenity that comes with a restful night. And let me assure you, as someone who has navigated the labyrinth of sleepless nights, there is a way out. There is a path to the peaceful sleep you crave, a way to align with the natural rhythms of your body and find solace in the quietude of the night.

Throughout these pages, I'll share not only research-backed strategies but also snippets of my journey, moments of vulnerability and triumph alike. We'll explore the intricacies of creating a sleep sanctuary, the dance between technology and tranquility, and the profound impact of small, consistent changes in our bedtime rituals.

So, dear reader, if you've ever felt the ache of exhaustion or the frustration of insomnia, know that you're in the right place. "The Art of Good Zzz's" is more than a book; it's a lifeline to the restorative power of sleep. Together.

Chapter 1

Understanding Insomnia

Defining Insomnia

"Insomnia" A word that echoes in the silence of the night. But what is it?

Insomnia is not just a lack of sleep. It's a relentless companion, a night-after-night struggle to find the elusive embrace of rest. It's the tug-of-war between mind and slumber, a battle we often feel powerless to win.

The Basics

Duration matters: Insomnia isn't just the occasional sleepless night. It's a persistent condition, lasting for weeks, even months.

Quality over quantity: It's not just about the hours in bed; it's about the quality of the sleep you get. Waking up groggy and unrested is a telltale sign.

The Impact

Hello, fatigue. Insomnia doesn't just stay in the bedroom. It follows you into the day, casting a shadow over your energy, focus, and mood.

Stress and insomnia: a vicious cycle. They dance together, each feeding off the other. Stress disrupts sleep, and lack of sleep fuels stress.

Personal Perspective

Imagine lying in bed, surrounded by darkness, the world asleep while you wrestle with your thoughts. That was me. Night after night. Tired but unable to find solace in sleep.

Real-World Insights
Insomnia Statistics:

According to the National Sleep Foundation, 30% of adults experience short-term insomnia.

Chronic insomnia affects about 10% of adults.

Clinical Insight:

Sleep studies show a link between chronic insomnia and increased risk of mental health issues.

Call-to-Action

1. **Sleep Diary:** Keep a simple sleep journal. Note bedtime, wake time, and how you feel in the morning. Patterns emerge, guiding your understanding.

2. **Create a Relaxing Pre-Sleep Routine:** Explore calming activities before bedtime. Whether it's reading a book, gentle stretching, or deep breathing, find what works for you.

3. **Limit Stimulants:** Cut down on caffeine and screen time before bed. Small changes here can have a big impact on your ability to unwind.

In the journey to overcome insomnia, these small steps pave the way for more restful nights. The road may be winding, but each step forward brings you closer to the peaceful slumber you deserve.

Common Causes of Insomnia

Insomnia, the silent thief of the night, can be triggered by various factors. Understanding these common causes is the first step towards regaining control over your sleep. Let's delve into the intricacies:

Stress and Anxiety

The Culprits: Everyday stressors, work pressure, or looming deadlines can make it difficult to silence the mind when it's time to sleep.

The Impact: Elevated stress hormones, like cortisol, interfere with the natural sleep process, leading to restless nights.

Disrupted Sleep Schedule

Irregular Bedtimes: Our bodies love routines. Inconsistent sleep and wake times disrupt the internal clock, making it harder to fall asleep.

Jet Lag and Shift Work: Crossing time zones or working odd hours confuses the body's natural circadian rhythm, leading to sleep-wake imbalances.

Poor Sleep Environment

Uncomfortable Bedding: An unsupportive mattress or lumpy pillows can turn a peaceful night into a battle of discomfort.

Light and Noise: A room resembling daylight or filled with noise can sabotage your sleep. Darkness and quiet are allies in the quest for rest.

Unhealthy Lifestyle Habits

Too Much Screen Time: The glow of screens before bedtime interferes with melatonin production, a hormone crucial for sleep.

Caffeine and Nicotine: Stimulants like coffee and nicotine can linger in the system, disrupting sleep even hours after consumption.

Medical Conditions

Chronic Pain: Conditions like arthritis or back pain can make finding a comfortable sleeping position a nightly challenge.

Mental Health Disorders: Depression and anxiety often intertwine with insomnia, creating a cycle that's hard to break.

Medications

Certain Prescription Drugs: Some medications, including those for hypertension or asthma, can interfere with sleep patterns.

Over-the-counter Medications: Even seemingly innocuous medications can contain stimulants that disrupt sleep.

Personal Experience

For me, it was the relentless pace of work and the glow of my phone in the dark. It took acknowledging these factors to begin my journey toward peaceful nights.*

Call-to-Action

1. **Stress Management:** Incorporate relaxation techniques such as deep breathing or meditation into your daily routine.

2. Establish a Consistent Sleep Schedule: Set a regular bedtime and wake-up time, even on weekends, to train your body's internal clock.

3. Evaluate Your Sleep Environment: Make your bedroom a sanctuary. Invest in comfortable bedding, and minimize light and noise for an optimal sleep haven.

Understanding these common causes is the key to reclaiming your nights. With awareness and targeted actions, you can break free from the shackles of insomnia and embrace the restful sleep you deserve.

The Link Between Stress and Sleep

In the intricate dance of night and day, stress can be a formidable disruptor, especially when it comes to the delicate art of sleep. Let's unravel the profound connection between stress and the restorative realm of slumber.

Stress Hormones and Sleep Disruption

Cortisol, the Culprit: Stress triggers the release of cortisol, a hormone designed for fight or flight. Unfortunately, elevated cortisol levels at bedtime can create a battleground instead of a haven for sleep.

Interrupted Sleep Cycles: The presence of cortisol can interfere with the progression of sleep cycles, leading to fragmented and unrestful nights.

Racing Thoughts and Insomnia

The Mind's Playground: Stress often translates into a racing mind, filled with worries, to-do lists, and hypothetical scenarios. This mental chatter becomes a persistent soundtrack when we should be entering the realm of dreams.

Insomnia's Ally: Chronic stress can be a loyal companion to insomnia, creating a cycle where the inability to sleep breeds more stress.

Physical Tension and Discomfort

Tense Muscles: Stress tightens muscles, setting the stage for physical discomfort that makes finding a comfortable sleep posture challenging.

Pain as a Consequence: Chronic stress can exacerbate conditions like tension headaches or back pain, making peaceful sleep an elusive prospect.

Sleep-Inducing Techniques

Deep Breathing: Calming the nervous system with slow, deep breaths signals to the body that it's time to relax.

Mindfulness Meditation: Cultivating a present-focused awareness can help to untangle the web of stress and ease the mind into a state conducive to sleep.

Real-World Insights

Consider this: A hectic day at work, deadlines looming, and an unresolved argument, sound familiar? This trifecta once defined my evenings, leaving me tossing and turning. Recognizing stress as the saboteur was the first step toward reclaiming my nights.*

Call-to-Action

1. Create a Wind-Down Routine: Establish a calming pre-sleep routine to signal to your body that it's time to unwind. This could include activities like reading a book, taking a warm bath, or practicing gentle stretching.

2. Journal Your Worries: Before bed, jot down your concerns or tasks for the next day. This simple act can offload the burden from your mind onto paper, easing mental tension.

3. Limit Stimulants Before Bed: Reduce caffeine and avoid stimulating activities close to bedtime. Opt for calming rituals instead to set the stage for restful sleep.

Chapter 2

Circadian Alignment

The Science of Circadian Rhythms

In the symphony of our existence, circadian rhythms compose the invisible yet powerful conductor orchestrating the ebb and flow of our daily lives. Understanding the science behind these internal timekeepers unveils the secrets to unlocking the art of circadian alignment.

What Are Circadian Rhythms?

Biological Clocks: Imagine tiny internal clocks ticking away, influencing everything from our sleep-wake cycles to hormone production.

24-Hour Cycle: Derived from the Latin words "circa diem" (around a day), circadian rhythms follow a roughly 24-hour cycle, syncing us with the Earth's rotation.

The Master Clock: The Suprachiasmatic Nucleus (SCN)

Located in the Brain: Nestled within the hypothalamus, the SCN acts as our internal timekeeper, receiving signals from light exposure to regulate our circadian rhythm.

Light as the Maestro: Natural light, especially in the morning, is the primary conductor of our circadian orchestra. It signals to the SCN that it's time to be awake and alert.

The Role of Melatonin

The Sleep Hormone: As the evening descends and darkness falls, the pineal gland releases melatonin, signaling to the body that it's time to wind down and prepare for sleep.

Blue Light's Influence: Artificial light, especially the blue light emitted by screens, can disrupt melatonin production, throwing our circadian rhythm out of tune.

Circadian Alignment and Sleep Quality

Impact on Sleep Architecture: When our circadian rhythms are in sync, we experience better-quality sleep with the right balance of REM (rapid eye movement) and deep sleep.

Mismatch and Consequences: Misalignments, like jet lag or irregular sleep schedules, can lead to sleep disturbances and impact overall well-being.

Real-World Insights

In my own journey to better sleep, understanding my circadian rhythm was a game-changer. It meant embracing the morning light, dimming the lights in the evening, and respecting the natural dance of day and night.

Call-to-Action

1. **Embrace Morning Light:** Spend time outdoors in the morning to signal to your body that it's time to be alert and awake.
2. **Dim the Lights at Night:** Create a soothing evening environment by reducing exposure to bright lights and avoiding screens at least an hour before bedtime.

3. Establish Consistent Sleep-Wake Times: Align your daily schedule with your natural circadian rhythm by maintaining consistent sleep and wake time, even on weekends.

Circadian alignment is the key to unlocking a harmonious relationship with sleep. By attuning ourselves to the natural cadence of our internal clocks, we pave the way for restful nights and energized days.

Strategies for Aligning Your Circadian Clock

In the intricate dance between our internal rhythms and the external world, aligning your circadian clock is akin to tuning an instrument for optimal performance. Here are practical strategies to harmonize your body's natural timekeeping:

1. Embrace Morning Light

The Morning Ritual: Spend time outdoors in the morning sunlight. This signals to your brain's internal clock that it's time to wake up and be alert.

Natural Light Exposure: If possible, aim for at least 20–30 minutes of natural light exposure in the early part of the day.

2. Set a Consistent Sleep Schedule

Routine is Key: Establish regular sleep and wake time. This consistency helps regulate your circadian rhythm, making it easier to fall asleep and wake up naturally.

Weekends Included: Try to maintain your sleep schedule even on weekends. Consistency reinforces your body's internal clock.

3. Control Light Exposure in the Evening

Dim the Lights: As evening approaches, reduce exposure to bright lights. Dim the lights in your home to signal to your body that bedtime is approaching.

Limit Screen Time: The blue light emitted by screens can suppress melatonin production. Minimize screen time at least an hour before bedtime.

4. Mind Your Meals

Eat Regularly: Consistent meal times can help regulate your body's internal clock. Avoid heavy meals close to bedtime.

Time Your Last Meal: Try to finish eating at least a few hours before bedtime to allow your body to focus on winding down.

5. Stay Active, but Time it Right

Morning Exercise: Engage in physical activity in the morning. This not only energizes you but also reinforces the daytime signal to your circadian clock.

Avoid Intense Exercise Before Bed: Vigorous exercise close to bedtime can be stimulating, potentially disrupting your ability to wind down.

6. Create a Relaxing Bedtime Ritual

Wind Down Activities: Develop calming pre-sleep rituals, such as reading a book, taking a warm bath, or practicing relaxation techniques.

Consistency is Calming: Engage in the same activities each night before bed. This repetition signals to your body that sleep is imminent.

7. Be Mindful of Naps

Limit Daytime Naps: If you nap during the day, keep it brief (20–30 minutes). Long naps or those taken too late in the day can interfere with nighttime sleep.

Early Afternoon Naps: If you feel the need to nap, aim for early afternoon to avoid disrupting your circadian rhythm.

8. Monitor Your Sleep Environment

Optimal Sleep Setting: Ensure your bedroom is conducive to sleep, cool, dark, and quiet. Invest in a comfortable mattress and pillows.

Limit Stimuli: Remove electronic devices from the bedroom and create a sanctuary free from distractions.

Call-to-Action

1. **Morning Sunlight Exposure:** Commit to spending time outdoors in the morning sunlight.

2. **Consistent Sleep Schedule:** Set a regular sleep and wake time, even on weekends.

3. **Evening Wind-Down Ritual:** Develop a calming pre-sleep routine to signal to your body that it's time to relax.

Importance of Consistent Sleep-Wake Times

In the rhythmic ballet of our daily lives, there's an often-overlooked maestro that orchestrates the harmony of our internal clocks: consistent sleep-wake times. Let's uncover the significance of this steady cadence and why it plays a pivotal role in the quality of our sleep and overall well-being.

1. Stability for Your Circadian Rhythm

Circadian Symphony: Our bodies thrive on routine. Consistent sleep and wake times synchronize with our internal circadian rhythm, optimizing the release of sleep-promoting hormones like melatonin.

Internal Clock Reinforcement: A regular schedule reinforces the natural ebb and flow of our body's biological processes, enhancing the predictability of when it's time to be alert and when it's time to wind down.

2. Improved Sleep Quality

Sleep Architecture: Consistent sleep-wake times contribute to the proper structure of sleep cycles, allowing for the progression through the essential stages of sleep, including deep, restorative rest.

Efficient Sleep Onset: When your body anticipates sleep at the same time each night, the process of falling asleep becomes more efficient, reducing the tossing and turning often associated with irregular sleep patterns.

3. Enhanced Daytime Alertness

Waking Up Refreshed: A regular wake time helps anchor your body clock, promoting a natural awakening that leaves you feeling refreshed and alert.

Reduced Morning Grogginess: Inconsistencies in wake times can lead to a phenomenon known as sleep inertia, that groggy feeling upon waking. Consistency minimizes this unwanted side effect.

4. Mood and Cognitive Benefits

Stable Mood Regulation: Regular sleep patterns contribute to stable mood regulation, reducing the likelihood of mood swings and irritability often associated with sleep disruption.

Cognitive Sharpness: A well-regulated sleep-wake schedule supports cognitive functions, enhancing memory, attention, and overall mental acuity.

5. Impact on Hormonal Balance

Hormonal Synchronization: Consistent sleep-wake times contribute to the synchronization of various hormones, including cortisol and insulin. This balance supports metabolic health and stress response.

Weight Regulation: Disruptions in sleep patterns can influence hunger hormones, potentially contributing to weight gain. A regular sleep routine supports healthy appetite regulation.

6. Resilience to Sleep Disorders

Insomnia Prevention: Establishing a consistent sleep schedule can be a powerful preventive measure against insomnia. It creates a stable framework that supports the body's natural sleep-wake rhythm.

Reduced Sleep Disorders: Consistency is a key ally in preventing and managing various sleep disorders, providing a foundation for improved sleep hygiene.

Call-to-Action

1. Set Regular Sleep and Wake Times: Commit to a consistent sleep and wake schedule, aligning with your body's natural circadian rhythm.

2. Create a Bedtime Routine: Develop calming pre-sleep rituals to signal to your body that it's time to wind down.

3. Limit Variations on Weekends: While flexibility is essential, try to minimize significant variations in your sleep-wake times, even on weekends.

Consistent sleep-wake times act as the stabilizing force in the ever-changing landscape of our lives. By embracing this rhythm, you not only enhance the quality of your sleep but also nurture a foundation for improved overall health and well-being. It's a small yet profound investment in the symphony of a balanced and energized life.

Chapter 3

Creating a Relaxing Sleep Environment

Optimal Bedroom Setup

In the pursuit of restful nights, your bedroom is more than just a physical space, it's your sanctuary, the canvas on which your dreams are painted. Let's delve into the art of crafting an optimal bedroom setup, where tranquility and comfort intertwine to create the perfect environment for rejuvenating sleep.

1. The Power of Darkness

Invest in Blackout Curtains: Block out intrusive light from street lamps or early morning sun. Darkness signals to your body that it's time to produce melatonin, the sleep hormone.

Eliminate Electronic Glows: Banish screens from your sleep haven. Even the soft glow of a charging device can interfere with your ability to drift into a peaceful slumber.

2. Temperature Harmony

Cool, Calm, and Collected: Maintain a cool bedroom temperature. A comfortable range is usually between 60-67 degrees Fahrenheit (15-20 degrees Celsius).

Layer Bedding for Control: Use layers on your bed so you can adjust according to your preference. A cozy blanket in cooler months and lighter sheets in the summer.

3. Mattress and Pillows Matter

Invest in Quality: Your mattress and pillows are the foundation of your sleep sanctuary. Choose a mattress that supports your spine and pillows that cradle your head comfortably.

Replace When Necessary: Mattresses and pillows have a lifespan. If they're sagging or lumpy, it's time for an upgrade.

4. Declutter for Serenity

Minimalism in Design: Simplify your bedroom design. A clutter-free space promotes a sense of calm, reducing visual distractions that can impede relaxation.

Organize Nightstands: Keep only essentials on your nightstand, such as a soothing book or a journal. Excessive items can create mental clutter.

5. Soothing Colors and Textures

Neutral Hues: Choose calming, neutral colors for your bedroom walls and bedding. Soft blues, greens, or earth tones can create a serene atmosphere.

Tactile Comfort: Incorporate textures that invite touch, a plush rug, smooth sheets, or a cozy throw blanket.

6. The Right Light

Soft, Warm Lighting: Opt for warm, soft lighting in the evening. Consider dimmer switches or bedside lamps to create a gradual transition to nighttime.

Limit Blue Light: Minimize exposure to blue light in the evening. Choose warm-toned bulbs and avoid screens at least an hour before bed.

7. Personal Touches

Aromatherapy: Explore calming scents like lavender or chamomile. Whether through essential oils, sachets, or candles, aromatherapy can promote relaxation.

Personalized Artwork: Display artwork or photographs that evoke positive emotions. Surround yourself with images that bring joy and calm.

Real-World Insights

For me, transforming my bedroom into a sleep haven was a game-changer. Soft lighting, blackout curtains, and a comfortable mattress turned my room into a retreat, signaling to my body that it was time to unwind.*

Call-to-Action

1. **Assess Your Bedroom Setup:** Evaluate your current sleep environment. Identify elements that may be disrupting your sleep or contributing to discomfort.

2. Implement Changes Gradually: Transforming your bedroom doesn't require a complete overhaul. Make small, gradual changes to create a space that resonates with tranquility.

3. Prioritize Comfort: Invest in quality bedding, consider blackout curtains, and pay attention to the details that contribute to a comfortable and calming atmosphere.

Crafting an optimal bedroom setup is a journey toward fostering an environment that embraces you in its soothing embrace, inviting the kind of restful sleep that restores both body and mind. It's a commitment to self-care that unfolds within the comforting walls of your sleep sanctuary.

Lighting and Its Impact on Sleep

In the intricate dance between light and darkness, our bodies are finely tuned to the cues provided by the changing illuminations of the day. Understanding the profound influence of lighting on our sleep-wake cycles unveils a key element in the quest for restful nights and energized days.

Natural Light: The Daytime Maestro

The Morning Cue: Exposure to natural light, especially in the morning, serves as a powerful signal to our internal clock that it's time to wake up and be alert.

Circadian Synchronization: Morning light exposure helps synchronize our circadian rhythm, regulating the release of melatonin, a hormone crucial for sleep-wake cycles.

Artificial Light and Its Dark Side

Blue Light Menace: Artificial lighting, particularly the blue light emitted by screens, can disrupt the delicate balance of our circadian rhythm.

Melatonin Suppression: Exposure to blue light in the evening suppresses melatonin production, tricking our bodies into thinking it's daytime and hindering the onset of sleep.

Strategies for Light Harmony

1. Embrace Morning Light

Outdoor Exposure: Spend time outdoors in the morning. Whether it's a brief walk or enjoying breakfast on the balcony, natural light kick-starts your body's alertness.

2. Mimic Natural Lighting Throughout the Day

Bright Light During the Day: If natural light is limited, consider using bright artificial lighting during the day to maintain circadian rhythm alignment.

Dim the Lights in the Evening: As evening approaches, transition to softer, warmer lighting to signal to your body that it's time to wind down.

3. Limit Blue Light in the Evening

Screen Time Awareness: Reduce screen time at least an hour before bedtime. If unavoidable, consider using blue light filters on electronic devices.

Blue Light Blocking Glasses: If you must use screens in the evening, consider wearing blue light-blocking glasses to mitigate the impact on melatonin production.

4. Invest in Smart Lighting Solutions

Adjustable Lighting: Invest in smart bulbs or lighting fixtures with adjustable color temperatures. This allows you to mimic natural light patterns throughout the day.

Programmable Timers: Use timers or smart home systems to gradually dim lights in the evening, creating a natural transition to bedtime.

Real-World Insights

In my journey to improve sleep, managing lighting was a game-changer. A morning walk became a ritual, and I embraced warm lighting in the evening, signaling to my body that it was time to relax.*

Call-to-Action

1. **Morning Light Ritual:** Incorporate a morning outdoor ritual. It could be as simple as sipping your morning coffee on the porch.

2. **Evening Light Transition:** Gradually dim lights in the evening to mimic the natural progression from day to night.

3. **Blue Light Awareness:** Limit screen time before bed and explore blue light filtering options for electronic devices.

By harnessing the power of light to align with our natural circadian rhythms, we not only optimize our sleep-wake cycles but also enhance our overall well-being. It's a conscious integration of lighting strategies that transform our living spaces into environments that support the restorative power of sleep.

Temperature and Sleep Quality

In the delicate ballet of achieving restful sleep, the temperature of your sleep environment plays a pivotal role. Just as Goldilocks sought the perfect porridge, finding the optimal temperature for your bedroom creates a sleep haven that promotes relaxation and rejuvenation.

The Goldilocks Zone: Not Too Hot, Not Too Cold

Ideal Temperature Range: Experts suggest maintaining a bedroom temperature between 60-67 degrees Fahrenheit (15-20 degrees Celsius) for optimal sleep.

Thermal Comfort: This temperature range supports thermal comfort, preventing excessive sweating or shivering during the night.

How Temperature Impacts Sleep Quality

1. Promoting Sleep Onset:

Cooling the Body: A slightly cooler environment can facilitate the natural drop in body temperature that occurs as you prepare for sleep, signaling to your body that it's time to wind down.

2. Sleep Architecture:

Deep Sleep Promotion: A cooler room can enhance the quality of deep sleep, allowing for the natural progression through sleep cycles.

Thermoregulation: The body's ability to regulate its temperature during sleep is crucial for maintaining the stability of sleep architecture.

3. Comfort for Your Sleep Sanctuary:

Bedding Adaptation: A cooler room allows you to layer bedding according to personal preference, ensuring comfort without overheating.

Create a Sleep Oasis: Tailor your sleep environment to be a cool, comfortable oasis that invites relaxation.

Strategies for Temperature Harmony

1. Adjust Bedding:

Layering: Use layers of blankets or sheets that can be easily adjusted. This allows you to regulate your body temperature without overheating.

Choose Breathable Fabrics: Opt for bedding made from breathable materials like cotton or linen, which facilitate airflow and heat dissipation.

2. Cooling Mattress and Pillows:

Technology Solutions: Consider mattresses and pillows designed with cooling technologies. Gel-infused memory foam or breathable materials can enhance temperature regulation.

3. Room Ventilation:

Airflow Enhancement: Ensure proper room ventilation. Fresh air circulation contributes to a comfortable sleep environment.

Use Fans Wisely: Ceiling fans or oscillating fans can be effective tools for maintaining airflow and creating a cool sleep atmosphere.

4. Thermal Regulation Pajamas:

Breathable Sleepwear: Choose lightweight, breathable sleepwear to support thermal comfort.

5. Smart Temperature Control:

Programmable Thermostats: If possible, use a programmable thermostat to adjust the room temperature automatically, creating a gradual cooling effect as bedtime approaches.

Real-World Insights

For me, discovering the impact of room temperature on sleep quality was transformative. Adjusting the thermostat and choosing breathable bedding turned my bedroom into a cocoon of comfort.

Call-to-Action

1. **Evaluate Your Bedroom Temperature:** Assess your current sleep environment and consider whether adjustments to the temperature could enhance your sleep quality.

2. Experiment with Bedding: Explore different types of bedding materials and layering options to find the combination that provides optimal comfort.

3. Incorporate Cooling Technologies: If needed, invest in mattresses or pillows designed to enhance temperature regulation for a more comfortable sleep experience.

By acknowledging the influence of temperature on sleep quality and implementing thoughtful strategies, you transform your bedroom into a haven that supports the peaceful and restorative sleep your body deserves. It's a simple yet powerful investment in the pursuit of a sleep sanctuary.

Chapter 4

The Role of Technology

Managing Screen Time Before Bed

In our digitally driven world, the glow of screens has become an integral part of our daily lives. However, understanding the impact of technology on our sleep is crucial for cultivating a healthy bedtime routine. Let's explore strategies for managing screen time before bed to foster a more restful and rejuvenating sleep experience.

1. The Blue Light Dilemma

Blue Light Suppression: Screens emit blue light, which suppresses the production of melatonin—the hormone responsible for signaling sleep.

Circadian Rhythm Disruption: Prolonged exposure to screens in the evening can disrupt the body's natural circadian rhythm, making it harder to transition into sleep mode.

2. Screen Time and Sleep Onset

Delayed Sleep Onset: Engaging with screens close to bedtime can delay the onset of sleep. The stimulating nature of content can keep the mind active when it should be winding down.

Impact on Relaxation: The constant influx of information from screens can heighten stress and anxiety, hindering the relaxation necessary for a smooth transition into sleep.

3. Strategies for Screen Time Management

a. Establish a Screen Curfew

Set a Time Limit: Designate a specific time before bed to power down electronic devices. Establishing a screen curfew helps signal to your body that it's time to unwind.

Gradual Reduction: If an abrupt cutoff is challenging, consider gradually reducing screen time in the hour leading up to bedtime.

b. Night Mode and Blue Light Filters

Night Mode Settings: Many devices offer night mode settings that reduce the emission of blue light in the evening. Enable these settings as bedtime approaches.

Blue Light Filters: Invest in blue light filters for screens or wear blue light-blocking glasses to mitigate the impact on melatonin production.

c. Create a Technology-Free Zone

Designate Screen-Free Spaces: Establish areas in your home, especially the bedroom, as technology-free zones. This promotes an environment conducive to relaxation and sleep.

Replace Screens with Relaxing Activities: Instead of scrolling through your phone, engage in calming activities like reading a physical book or practicing mindfulness.

d. Explore Sleep-Inducing Apps

Guided Meditation Apps: If you choose to use technology before bed, explore apps that offer guided meditations or soothing sounds to promote relaxation.

Digital Bedtime Stories: Some apps provide digital bedtime stories, offering a screen alternative that fosters a sense of calm.

Real-World Insights

Recognizing the impact of screen time on my sleep, I implemented a screen curfew and replaced evening scrolling with a calming bedtime routine. The result? A noticeable improvement in the quality of my sleep.*

Call-to-Action

1. Evaluate Your Screen Time Habits: Reflect on your current screen time habits, especially in the hour before bedtime. Identify areas for improvement.

2. Establish a Screen Curfew: Set a specific time to power down electronic devices, gradually reducing screen exposure as bedtime approaches.

3. Explore Blue Light Filters: Investigate the availability of night mode settings on your devices or invest in blue light filters to minimize the impact on melatonin production.

Sleep-Inducing Apps and Gadgets

In the quest for restful nights, technology can transition from being a potential disruptor to a valuable ally. Sleep-inducing apps and gadgets harness the power of innovation to guide us into a serene and rejuvenating slumber. Let's explore the digital tools designed to enhance the quality of our sleep.

Sleep-Inducing Apps

1. Guided Meditation Apps:

Calm: Offering guided meditations and relaxing sounds, Calm helps ease the mind and promote a sense of tranquility before bedtime.

Headspace: Known for its mindfulness exercises, Headspace provides sleepcasts and calming stories to lull you into a peaceful sleep.

2. Relaxing Sound Apps:

White Noise Lite: Customizable with a variety of soothing sounds, White Noise Lite can drown out background noise, creating a peaceful auditory environment.

Rain Rain Sleep Sounds: Bringing the calming ambiance of rain, this app offers a selection of rain sounds to induce relaxation.

3. Digital Bedtime Stories:

Calm and Headspace (Again): In addition to meditation, these apps feature bedtime stories narrated by soothing voices, designed to guide you into dreamland.

Audible: While not exclusively a sleep app, Audible offers an extensive collection of audiobooks, including many narrated with a calming tone ideal for bedtime.

4. Sleep Tracking Apps:

Sleep Cycle: Analyzing your sleep patterns, Sleep Cycle wakes you during your lightest sleep phase, enhancing the feeling of waking up naturally.

Pillow: Combining sleep tracking with a smart alarm, Pillow provides insights into your sleep cycles and offers tools for better sleep hygiene.

Sleep-Inducing Gadgets

1. Smart Lighting Systems:

Philips Hue: Programmable to mimic natural light patterns, Philips Hue smart bulbs can be set to gradually dim in the evening, signaling to your body that it's time to wind down.

Casper Glow Light: Specifically designed for bedtime, this bedside lamp emits a warm, dimming light to help ease the transition from wakefulness to sleep.

2. White Noise Machines:

Marpac Dohm White Noise Machine: Producing a constant, soothing sound, this mechanical white noise machine helps drown out disturbances that may disrupt sleep.

Adaptive Sound Technologies LectroFan: Offering a variety of white noise and fan sounds, this compact device is suitable for home or travel.

3. Smart Mattress and Sleep Trackers:

Eight Sleep Pod: Equipped with temperature control, the Eight Sleep Pod adjusts the bed's temperature to enhance comfort and promote better sleep.

Withings Sleep Analyzer: Placed under the mattress, this sleep tracker monitors sleep cycles, heart rate, and snoring, providing comprehensive insights into your sleep patterns.

Real-World Insights

In my journey to better sleep, incorporating sleep-inducing apps and gadgets became a game-changer. Guided meditation and calming sounds transformed my bedtime routine, creating a serene atmosphere conducive to rest.*

Call-to-Action

1. **Explore Sleep Apps:** Experiment with different sleep-inducing apps to find the ones that resonate with your preferences and contribute to a calming bedtime routine.

2. Consider Smart Lighting: Invest in smart lighting systems that allow you to customize your bedroom's lighting to promote relaxation in the evening.

3. Evaluate Sleep Gadgets: Explore sleep gadgets such as white noise machines or sleep trackers to understand how they may enhance your sleep environment and quality.

By leveraging the benefits of sleep-inducing apps and gadgets, you can tailor your bedtime routine to match your preferences and foster an environment conducive to restful sleep. Embrace the innovation that technology offers in the realm of sleep, transforming your nightly rituals into a peaceful and rejuvenating experience.

Sleep-inducing apps and gadgets harness the power of innovation to guide us into a serene and rejuvenating slumber.

Chapter 5

Healthy Bedtime Routines

Establishing a Pre-Sleep Ritual

In the cadence of a restful night lies the symphony of a well-crafted bedtime routine. A pre-sleep ritual serves as the gentle conductor, guiding you from the hustle of the day into the serenity of the night. Let's explore the elements that contribute to a healthy bedtime routine, fostering an environment primed for restorative sleep.

1. Wind Down Activities

Reading a Book: Engaging with a physical book, preferably one that doesn't stimulate the mind excessively, can be a calming way to transition into bedtime.

Journaling: Reflecting on the day in a journal helps release lingering thoughts and allows for a mental winding down.

2. Limit Stimulants

Caffeine Awareness: Be mindful of your caffeine intake, especially in the hours leading up to bedtime. Opt for decaffeinated options if you desire a warm beverage.

Avoid Heavy Meals: Consuming heavy or spicy meals close to bedtime can cause discomfort and disrupt sleep.

3. Screen Curfew

Establish a Screen Curfew: Power down electronic devices at least an hour before bed. The blue light emitted by screens can suppress melatonin production, hindering the onset of sleep.

Engage in Screen-Free Activities: Replace screen time with activities that promote relaxation, such as gentle stretching or listening to calming music.

4. Create a Relaxing Environment

Dim the Lights: Transition to soft, warm lighting in the evening to signal to your body that it's time to wind down.

Use Aromatherapy: Incorporate calming scents, such as lavender or chamomile, through essential oils or scented candles.

5. Gentle Stretching or Yoga

Release Tension: Engage in gentle stretching or yoga poses to release physical tension accumulated during the day.

Focus on Breathing: Incorporate deep, mindful breathing exercises to calm the nervous system.

6. Consistent Sleep Schedule

Set a Regular Sleep Time: Establish a consistent bedtime that allows for an adequate duration of sleep. Consistency reinforces your body's internal clock.

Wake Up at the Same Time: Aim to wake up at the same time each day, even on weekends. This consistency helps regulate your sleep-wake cycle.

7. Hydration Management

Hydrate Mindfully: While staying hydrated is essential, try to limit excessive fluid intake close to bedtime to avoid disruptions due to bathroom visits.

Herbal Tea Option: Consider herbal teas with calming properties, such as chamomile or peppermint, as part of your evening routine.

Real-World Insights

In my journey to establish a healthy bedtime routine, I prioritized winding down activities and created a screen curfew. These simple yet intentional choices transformed my evenings and significantly improved my sleep quality.

Call-to-Action

1. **Assess Your Current Routine:** Reflect on your current bedtime habits and identify areas for improvement.

2. **Experiment with Wind Down Activities:** Explore different activities to incorporate into your pre-sleep ritual, such as reading, journaling, or gentle stretching.

3. Establish Consistency: Set a regular sleep time and wake-up time to create a consistent sleep schedule. Consistency is key in reinforcing your body's internal clock.

By weaving these elements into your pre-sleep ritual, you craft a bedtime routine uniquely tailored to your needs. A healthy bedtime routine becomes a cherished companion, guiding you gently into the embrace of restful sleep and setting the stage for waking up refreshed and rejuvenated.

Relaxation Techniques for Better Sleep

In the hustle and bustle of modern life, the ability to unwind is a precious skill that directly impacts the quality of our sleep. Incorporating relaxation techniques into your bedtime routine can serve as a bridge between the demands of the day and the serenity of the night. Let's explore effective relaxation techniques that pave the way for a restful and rejuvenating sleep experience.

1. Progressive Muscle Relaxation (PMR)

Method: Start by tensing and then gradually releasing each muscle group, moving from toes to head. Focus on the sensation of relaxation as tension dissipates.

Purpose: PMR promotes physical relaxation, releasing tension from the body and calming the nervous system.

2. Mindful Breathing

Technique: Practice deep, diaphragmatic breathing. Inhale slowly through your nose, allowing your abdomen to expand, then exhale slowly through your mouth.

Purpose: Mindful breathing activates the body's relaxation response, lowering stress hormones and promoting a sense of calm.

3. Guided Imagery and Visualization

Guidance: Envision a tranquil scene or follow a guided imagery script. Imagine the sights, sounds, and sensations of a peaceful place.

Purpose: Guided imagery redirects your focus away from stressors, fostering a calming mental environment conducive to sleep.

4. Body Scan Meditation

Process: Mentally scan your body from head to toe, paying attention to any areas of tension or discomfort. Release tension as you bring awareness to each part.

Purpose: Body scan meditation promotes awareness of physical sensations, facilitating relaxation and easing the transition into sleep.

5. Autogenic Training

Affirmations: Repeat a series of calming, self-generated phrases silently. For example, "My arms are heavy, and warm," fostering a sense of relaxation.

Purpose: Autogenic training promotes a state of physiological calmness, signaling to the body that it's time to wind down.

6. Calming Visualization

Imagery: Picture a serene scene, such as a beach at sunset or a peaceful garden. Engage all your senses in this mental retreat.

Purpose: Calming visualization distracts the mind from stressors, creating a mental space conducive to relaxation.

7. Yoga Nidra

Practice: Also known as yogic sleep, this practice involves guided meditation in a comfortable lying-down position, focusing on body awareness and breath.

Purpose: Yoga Nidra induces a state of deep relaxation, promoting both mental and physical tranquility.

8. Aromatherapy

Scents: Experiment with calming scents such as lavender, chamomile, or bergamot. Use essential oils, diffusers, or scented pillows.

Purpose: Aromatherapy engages the olfactory senses, triggering a relaxation response and creating a soothing sleep environment.

Real-World Insights

Incorporating relaxation techniques into my nightly routine transformed my approach to sleep. Mindful breathing and guided imagery became anchors, signaling to my body that it was time to unwind.

Call-to-Action

1. **Explore Techniques:** Experiment with different relaxation techniques to identify those that resonate with you. Consider incorporating a variety into your bedtime routine.

2. Consistency Matters: Make relaxation a consistent part of your routine. Repetition reinforces the effectiveness of these techniques in signaling the body that it's time to relax.

3. Create a Relaxation Space: Designate a calm, quiet space for your relaxation practice. Minimize distractions to enhance the effectiveness of these techniques.

By embracing these relaxation techniques, you equip yourself with powerful tools to navigate the transition from the demands of the day to the tranquility of sleep. Integrating these practices into your bedtime routine sets the stage for a more restful and rejuvenating night's sleep.

The Power of Mindfulness and Meditation

In the midst of our fast-paced lives, the ancient practices of mindfulness and meditation emerge as potent tools for cultivating a sense of inner calm and promoting overall well-being. As we navigate the complexities of the modern world, the power of these practices becomes increasingly evident, especially in the realm of improving sleep quality and fostering a deeper connection with our inner selves.

1. Understanding Mindfulness

Present-Moment Awareness: Mindfulness involves being fully present and engaged in the current moment, acknowledging thoughts and feelings without judgment.

Cultivating Observant Attention: Through mindfulness, we develop the ability to observe our thoughts and sensations with curiosity, fostering a non-reactive and accepting mindset.

2. The Essence of Meditation

Focused Attention: Meditation, in its various forms, often centers around focused attention, whether on the breath, a mantra, or a specific point of focus.

Inner Exploration: Meditation provides a space for inner exploration, allowing thoughts to arise and pass without attachment or distraction.

3. Impact on Sleep Quality

Stress Reduction: Mindfulness and meditation are renowned for reducing stress levels, which is often a significant contributor to sleep disturbances.

Calming the Mind: These practices create a mental environment conducive to relaxation, helping to alleviate the racing thoughts that can interfere with sleep.

4. Mindfulness-Based Stress Reduction (MBSR)

Structured Approach: MBSR, developed by Dr. Jon Kabat-Zinn, combines mindfulness meditation and yoga to enhance awareness and reduce stress.

Clinical Applications: MBSR has been incorporated into clinical settings and is recognized for its efficacy in managing various conditions, including insomnia.

5. Meditation for Sleep

Guided Sleep Meditations: Purposeful meditation sessions designed for bedtime often incorporate elements of relaxation, body awareness, and visualization.

Enhanced Sleep Induction: By calming the mind and body, meditation serves as a powerful aid in facilitating the transition into a restful sleep state.

6. Practical Tips for Mindfulness and Meditation

Start Small: Begin with short sessions, gradually extending the duration as your practice deepens.

Consistency Matters: Regular, consistent practice amplifies the benefits of mindfulness and meditation.

Integrate into Daily Life: Infuse moments of mindfulness into daily activities, such as mindful eating or mindful walking.

Utilize Resources: Explore guided meditations, and mindfulness apps, or attend meditation classes to support your practice.

Real-World Insights

Incorporating mindfulness into my daily routine was transformative. A short mindfulness pause before bed became a beacon of calm, preparing me for a more peaceful night's sleep.

Call-to-Action

1. **Start Today:** Begin your mindfulness and meditation journey with a brief session. Even a few minutes can make a difference.

2. **Explore Techniques:** Experiment with various meditation techniques, such as mindfulness meditation, loving-kindness meditation, or body scan meditation, to discover what resonates with you.

3. **Build Consistency:** Make mindfulness and meditation a regular part of your routine. Consistency is key to experiencing the full benefits of these practices.

Chapter 6

Nutrition and Sleep

Foods That Promote Sleep

In the intricate dance of sleep, the role of nutrition cannot be overstated. The foods we consume play a pivotal role in influencing the quality of our sleep. Let's explore a palette of nourishing choices that can become allies in the quest for restful nights and rejuvenated mornings.

1. Cherries and Cherry Products

Melatonin Boost: Cherries are a natural source of melatonin, the hormone that regulates sleep-wake cycles. Consider incorporating fresh cherries, cherry juice, or dried cherries into your evening routine.

2. Fatty Fish: Salmon, Tuna, and Mackerel

Omega-3 Fatty Acids: Rich in omega-3 fatty acids, these fish varieties are associated with enhanced sleep quality. Omega-3s may increase the production of serotonin, a neurotransmitter linked to sleep regulation.

Vitamin D: Fatty fish are also a natural source of vitamin D, which plays a role in regulating sleep.

3. Nuts and Seeds: Almonds, Walnuts, Chia Seeds

Magnesium Content: Nuts and seeds, particularly almonds and walnuts, are rich in magnesium, a mineral that may promote relaxation and support sleep.

Tryptophan Presence: Some nuts, like almonds, contain tryptophan, an amino acid precursor to serotonin and melatonin.

4. Kiwi

Serotonin Boost: Kiwi is not only a rich source of antioxidants but also contains serotonin precursors. Consuming kiwi in the evening may contribute to better sleep.

5. Herbal Teas: Chamomile and Valerian Root

Calming Properties: Chamomile tea is renowned for its calming effects, promoting relaxation and potentially improving sleep quality.

Valerian Root: Valerian root, often brewed as tea, has been traditionally used as a natural remedy for insomnia.

6. Warm Milk

Tryptophan and Calcium Combo: Warm milk is a classic bedtime beverage that combines the sleep-promoting effects of tryptophan and the calming properties of calcium.

7. Whole Grains: Quinoa, Barley, Brown Rice

Complex Carbohydrates: Whole grains contain complex carbohydrates that may increase serotonin production, contributing to a sense of relaxation.

Fiber Content: The fiber in whole grains can help regulate blood sugar levels, preventing disruptions that might interfere with sleep.

8. Herbal Supplements: Lavender and Passionflower
Relaxing Effects: Herbal supplements like lavender and passionflower are believed to have relaxing properties, potentially aiding in sleep induction.

Real-World Insights

Transforming my evening snack routine to include a small bowl of cherries and a handful of almonds made a noticeable difference in my sleep quality. These simple additions became my delicious allies in the pursuit of restful nights.

Call-to-Action

1. Explore and Experiment: Integrate sleep-promoting foods into your evening routine and observe their impact on your sleep quality.

2. Create Nutrient-Rich Snacks: Craft bedtime snacks that combine sleep-enhancing ingredients, such as a small bowl of cherries with a handful of nuts or a calming cup of herbal tea.

3. Mindful Consumption: Be mindful of portion sizes, especially close to bedtime, to prevent discomfort and indigestion.

Timing of Meals for Optimal Sleep

In the intricate tapestry of sleep hygiene, the timing of meals emerges as a crucial thread. When and what we eat can significantly impact our ability to drift into restful slumber. Let's delve into the importance of meal timing and its role in fostering optimal sleep.

1. The Digestive Dance

Digestion and Sleep: The digestive process requires energy, and consuming large or heavy meals close to bedtime can divert energy toward digestion when the body should be transitioning into sleep mode.

Avoid Late-Night Feasts: Overeating or indulging in heavy, rich foods late at night can lead to discomfort, and indigestion, and may disrupt the natural progression into sleep.

2. The Blood Sugar Balancing Act

Blood Sugar Levels: Eating a meal that causes a rapid spike in blood sugar levels, especially close to bedtime, can result in fluctuations that may disturb sleep.

Balanced Meals: Aim for balanced meals that include a combination of complex carbohydrates, protein, and healthy fats to help regulate blood sugar levels.

3. Timing and Melatonin Release

Melatonin Production: Melatonin, the hormone that regulates sleep-wake cycles, is influenced by our body's internal clock, known as the circadian rhythm.

Meal Timing and Melatonin: Consuming meals at irregular times, especially late at night, can disrupt the natural release of melatonin, potentially affecting the onset of sleep.

4. Evening Snacks Done Right

Light and Nutrient-Rich: If hunger strikes before bedtime, opt for light, nutrient-rich snacks. Consider combinations like yogurt with berries, a small bowl of cherries, or a handful of nuts.

Avoid Stimulants: Steer clear of caffeinated beverages or foods with high caffeine content in the hours leading up to bedtime.

5. Hydration and Bedtime

Hydration Balance: Staying adequately hydrated is crucial, but excessive fluid intake close to bedtime may lead to disruptions from frequent trips to the bathroom.

Limit Stimulating Drinks: Minimize the consumption of caffeinated beverages and opt for calming, caffeine-free options like herbal tea.

6. Meal Timing Strategies

Regular Meal Schedule: Establish a consistent meal schedule to align with your body's internal clock. Regularity reinforces the circadian rhythm and supports overall sleep quality.

Dinner Timing: Aim to have dinner at least 2-3 hours before bedtime, allowing for adequate digestion before sleep.

Real-World Insights

Shifting my dinner to an earlier time and opting for a light evening snack made a noticeable difference in my sleep quality. These adjustments aligned my meal timing with my body's natural rhythm.

Call-to-Action

1. Assess Your Current Meal Timing: Reflect on your current meal schedule and identify areas for adjustment, especially in the evening.

2. Establish Consistent Meal Times: Set regular meal times to support your body's circadian rhythm. Consistency reinforces the body's internal clock.

3. Choose Light Evening Snacks: If hunger strikes before bedtime, choose light, nutrient-dense snacks that won't overload your digestive system.

By paying attention to the timing of your meals, you synchronize your eating habits with your body's internal clock, promoting a seamless transition into restful sleep. It's a mindful integration of nutrition and circadian rhythm that contributes to the symphony of a good night's rest.

Chapter 7

Physical Activity and Sleep

The Connection Between Exercise and Sleep

In the dance between physical activity and sleep, each step contributes to the harmony of a restful night. Understanding the profound connection between exercise and sleep unveils a powerful tool for optimizing both physical well-being and the quality of our nightly repose.

1. The Exercise-Sleep Symbiosis

Reciprocal Relationship: Regular physical activity establishes a reciprocal relationship with sleep, influencing its duration and quality.

Enhanced Sleep Quality: Engaging in exercise, whether aerobic or resistance training, has been associated with improved sleep quality and efficiency.

2. Timing Matters: The Exercise-Sleep Equation

Daytime Benefits: Physical activity during the day contributes to increased energy expenditure, promoting a sense of fatigue that aids in falling asleep more easily at night.

Avoid Intense Evening Workouts: While exercise is generally beneficial, intense workouts close to bedtime may elevate heart rate and body temperature, potentially hindering the onset of sleep.

3. The Impact of Exercise Types

Aerobic Exercise: Activities like jogging, swimming, or cycling are linked to improved sleep duration and quality. Aim for at least 150 minutes of moderate-intensity aerobic exercise per week.

Resistance Training: Incorporating resistance training, such as weightlifting, enhances sleep parameters and may contribute to a more robust sleep routine.

4. *The Stress-Reducing Effect*

Stress Reduction: Exercise serves as a potent stress reducer, helping to alleviate anxiety and tension that can interfere with the ability to fall asleep.

Cortisol Regulation: Physical activity contributes to the regulation of cortisol, a stress hormone, promoting a more balanced and harmonious internal environment.

5. *Consistency and Routine*

Establish a Routine: Consistency is key. Establishing a regular exercise routine, ideally earlier in the day, supports the synchronization of your body's internal clock.

Mindful Evening Activities: If exercising in the evening, opt for calming activities like yoga or gentle stretching to wind down the body.

6. *Real-World Insights*

Incorporating regular exercise into my routine not only elevated my daytime energy levels but also ushered in more profound and rejuvenating sleep. The synergy between physical activity and sleep transformed my overall well-being.*

Call-to-Action

1. **Evaluate Your Exercise Routine:** Reflect on your current exercise habits and their potential impact on your sleep quality.

2. **Establish Consistency:** If not already part of your routine, consider incorporating regular physical activity into your schedule. Choose activities you enjoy to enhance adherence.

3. **Mindful Evening Workouts:** If exercising in the evening, opt for activities that promote relaxation rather than intensity. Observe how this influences your sleep patterns.

By recognizing the intricate connection between physical activity and sleep, you harness a dynamic duo for fostering holistic well-being. Whether through the invigorating rhythm of aerobic exercise or the strength-building cadence of resistance training, each step contributes to the symphony of a good night's sleep. It's a harmonious partnership that transcends the realms of movement and rest, laying the foundation for a healthier and more rejuvenated you.

Creating a Balanced Exercise Routine

In the pursuit of optimal health, a balanced exercise routine stands as a cornerstone, offering a holistic approach to fitness that not only enhances physical well-being but also contributes to mental and emotional vitality. Let's explore the key principles and considerations for crafting a well-rounded and sustainable exercise regimen.

1. Variety in Modalities

Incorporate Cardiovascular Exercise: Activities like jogging, cycling, or swimming elevate heart rate, enhance cardiovascular health, and contribute to overall endurance.

Integrate Strength Training: Resistance exercises, using weights or bodyweight, build muscle strength, improve metabolism, and support joint health.

Include Flexibility and Mobility Work: Incorporating activities like yoga or dynamic stretching promotes flexibility, reduces the risk of injury, and contributes to overall mobility.

2. Frequency and Consistency

Establish Regularity: Aim for at least 150 minutes of moderate-intensity aerobic exercise per week or 75 minutes of vigorous-intensity exercise. Include strength training at least two days per week.

Spread Activities Throughout the Week: Distribute exercise sessions across the week to allow for adequate recovery and reduce the risk of burnout.

3. Individualization and Enjoyment

Consider Personal Preferences: Choose activities that align with your interests and preferences. Enjoyment increases the likelihood of adherence to a routine.

Individualize Intensity: Tailor the intensity of workouts based on your fitness level. Gradually progress to more challenging exercises to avoid burnout or injury.

4. Recovery and Rest Days

Prioritize Recovery: Allow time for your body to recover between intense workouts. Adequate rest is crucial for muscle repair and overall recovery.

Incorporate Rest Days: Designate at least one or two rest days per week to prevent overtraining and promote overall well-being.

5. Listen to Your Body

Pay Attention to Signals: Be attuned to your body's signals. If you experience persistent fatigue, soreness, or pain, consider adjusting the intensity or type of exercise.

Modify as Needed: Modify your routine based on changes in fitness level, health status, or life circumstances. Flexibility is key to a sustainable exercise regimen.

6. Progression and Goal Setting

Set Realistic Goals: Define clear and achievable fitness goals. Whether it's improving endurance, building muscle, or enhancing flexibility, having specific objectives provides motivation.

Gradual Progression: Progress gradually to avoid overexertion. Incrementally increase intensity, duration, or complexity to challenge your body while minimizing the risk of injury.

7. Mind-Body Connection

Include Mindful Practices: Integrate mindfulness into your routine through activities like yoga or tai chi. These practices not only enhance physical flexibility but also promote mental relaxation.

Prioritize Stress Management: Recognize the role of exercise in stress reduction. Balancing high-intensity workouts with calming activities contributes to overall stress management.

Real-World Insights

Crafting a balanced exercise routine transformed my approach to fitness. The integration of strength training, cardiovascular exercise, and mindful practices created a comprehensive regimen that I genuinely enjoyed.

Call-to-Action

1. Assess Your Current Routine: Reflect on your current exercise habits. Identify areas for improvement or modification based on your goals and preferences.

2. Diversify Your Activities: Introduce variety into your routine by incorporating different types of exercise. This not only enhances overall fitness but also prevents monotony.

3. Prioritize Enjoyment: Choose activities that bring you joy. Whether it's dancing, hiking, or playing a sport, the more you enjoy your workouts, the more likely you are to stick with them.

By weaving these principles into the fabric of your exercise routine, you cultivate a holistic approach that nurtures not only physical strength but also mental resilience and emotional well-being. A balanced exercise regimen becomes a sustainable and enjoyable journey towards overall health and vitality.

Chapter 8

Sleep Disorders and Their Solutions

Overview of Common Sleep Disorders

In the realm of sleep, a spectrum of disorders can cast shadows over the tranquility of the night. Understanding these sleep disorders is pivotal for recognizing symptoms, seeking appropriate solutions, and reclaiming the restful nights essential for overall well-being. Let's explore some prevalent sleep disorders and potential solutions.

1. Insomnia

Characteristics: Persistent difficulty falling asleep, staying asleep, or experiencing non-restorative sleep.

Common Causes: Stress, anxiety, depression, lifestyle factors, or underlying medical conditions.

Solutions:

Cognitive Behavioral Therapy for Insomnia (CBT-I): A structured therapeutic approach that addresses thoughts and behaviors contributing to insomnia.

Sleep Hygiene Practices: Establishing a consistent sleep schedule, creating a relaxing bedtime routine, and optimizing the sleep environment.

Medications: In some cases, medications may be prescribed for short-term relief. However, they should be used under the guidance of a healthcare professional.

2. Sleep Apnea

Characteristics: Periodic pauses in breathing during sleep, often accompanied by loud snoring.

Common Causes: Obstructive sleep apnea is typically related to airway obstruction, while central sleep apnea results from a failure of the brain to send proper signals to the muscles controlling breathing.

Solutions:

Continuous Positive Airway Pressure (CPAP): A common treatment involving a machine that delivers a continuous flow of air to keep the airway open.

Bi-level Positive Airway Pressure (BiPAP): Similar to CPAP but provides different air pressure levels for inhalation and exhalation.

Lifestyle Changes: Weight loss, positional therapy, and avoiding alcohol and sedatives before bedtime.

3. Restless Legs Syndrome (RLS)

Characteristics: Unpleasant sensations in the legs, often accompanied by an irresistible urge to move them for relief.

Common Causes: Genetic factors, iron deficiency, peripheral neuropathy, or pregnancy.

Solutions:

Medications: Dopaminergic agents, anticonvulsants, or opioids may be prescribed to alleviate symptoms.

Iron Supplements: If iron deficiency is identified, supplementation may be recommended.

Lifestyle Changes: Regular exercise, avoiding stimulants, and establishing a consistent sleep routine.

4. Narcolepsy

Characteristics: Excessive daytime sleepiness, sudden muscle weakness (cataplexy), and episodes of sleep paralysis or hallucinations.

Common Causes: Abnormalities in the brain's regulation of sleep-wake cycles.

Solutions:

Stimulant Medications: To improve wakefulness and alertness during the day.

Selective Serotonin and Norepinephrine Reuptake Inhibitors (SSNRIs): To manage symptoms of cataplexy and improve nighttime sleep.

5. Parasomnias

Characteristics: Abnormal behaviors during sleep, such as sleepwalking, night terrors, or sleep-related eating disorder.

Common Causes: Often associated with disruptions in the sleep cycle or underlying medical conditions.

Solutions:

Creating a Safe Sleep Environment: Minimizing potential hazards for those who experience sleepwalking or night terrors.

Behavioral Interventions: In some cases, cognitive-behavioral therapy may be beneficial.

Real-World Insights

Navigating insomnia, I discovered the effectiveness of CBT-I techniques, transforming my relationship with sleep. Understanding and addressing sleep disorders became a crucial step in reclaiming restful nights.

Call-to-Action

1. Recognize Symptoms: Be attentive to signs of sleep disorders, such as persistent difficulties falling asleep, excessive daytime sleepiness, or unusual behaviors during sleep.

2. Consult a Professional: If sleep issues persist, consult with a healthcare professional or a sleep specialist for a comprehensive evaluation and diagnosis.

3. Explore Treatment Options: Collaborate with healthcare providers to explore appropriate treatment options, which may include lifestyle modifications, therapy, or medications.

By shedding light on common sleep disorders and their potential solutions, this chapter aims to empower individuals to recognize, seek help, and implement strategies that foster restorative and rejuvenating sleep.

Treatment Options and Strategies

Embarking on the journey to better sleep involves a multifaceted approach that considers lifestyle adjustments, therapeutic interventions, and, in some cases, medical treatments. This chapter explores a range of treatment options and strategies designed to address various sleep challenges, empowering individuals to tailor their approach based on their unique needs.

1. Sleep Hygiene Practices

Consistent Sleep Schedule: Establishing a regular sleep schedule, going to bed, and waking up at the same time every day, reinforces the body's internal clock.

Optimal Sleep Environment: Create a comfortable and conducive sleep environment by regulating room temperature, minimizing noise and light, and investing in a comfortable mattress and pillows.

Bedtime Routine: Develop a relaxing pre-sleep routine to signal to your body that it's time to wind down. This may include activities like reading, gentle stretching, or practicing relaxation techniques.

2. Cognitive Behavioral Therapy for Insomnia (CBT-I)

Addressing Negative Thoughts: CBT-I targets thoughts and behaviors that contribute to insomnia. It helps individuals identify and change negative thought patterns related to sleep.

Sleep Restriction: A component of CBT-I involves limiting the time spent in bed awake, helping to consolidate sleep and improve overall sleep efficiency.

Stimulus Control: Techniques to associate the bed and bedroom with sleep, breaking the connection with activities that may interfere with sleep.

3. Relaxation Techniques

Progressive Muscle Relaxation (PMR): Systematically tensing and then relaxing muscle groups to promote physical relaxation.

Mindfulness Meditation: Engaging in mindfulness practices, such as deep breathing or guided meditation, to calm the mind and reduce stress.

Yoga and Tai Chi: Incorporating gentle, mindful movement practices that promote relaxation and enhance flexibility.

4. Sleep Medications

Short-Term Use: In some cases, healthcare providers may prescribe sleep medications for short-term relief. These may include sedative-hypnotics or medications that target specific sleep disorders.

Caution and Monitoring: Sleep medications should be used under the guidance of a healthcare professional, and their use requires careful monitoring due to the potential for dependence and side effects.

5. Continuous Positive Airway Pressure (CPAP) Therapy

For Sleep Apnea: CPAP therapy involves using a machine that delivers a continuous stream of air to keep the airway open during sleep.

Adherence and Comfort: Proper fit, regular maintenance, and ensuring comfort are crucial for adherence to CPAP therapy.

6. Lifestyle Modifications

Regular Exercise: Engaging in regular physical activity, preferably earlier in the day, contributes to overall well-being and can positively impact sleep.

Healthy Diet: Adopting a balanced and nutritious diet supports overall health, including sleep. Limiting caffeine and avoiding heavy meals close to bedtime can be beneficial.

Stress Management: Incorporating stress-reducing practices, such as mindfulness, relaxation techniques, or hobbies, can mitigate the impact of stress on sleep.

7. Professional Guidance and Sleep Specialists

Consulting Healthcare Professionals: Seeking guidance from healthcare providers, sleep specialists, or mental health professionals can provide personalized insights and recommendations.

Sleep Studies: In cases of suspected sleep disorders, undergoing a sleep study (polysomnography) may be recommended to diagnose and understand the specific nature of the sleep challenge.

Real-World Insights

Combining CBT-I techniques, relaxation practices, and lifestyle adjustments transformed my approach to sleep. The integration of various strategies personalized to my needs became the foundation of my restful nights.

Call-to-Action

1. **Self-Assessment:** Reflect on your current sleep habits, noting any persistent challenges or patterns that may indicate a sleep disorder.

2. **Explore Strategies:** Experiment with different strategies, such as sleep hygiene practices, relaxation techniques, or CBT-I principles, to identify what works best for you.

3. **Consult Professionals:** If sleep issues persist or worsen, consult with healthcare professionals or sleep specialists for a thorough evaluation and personalized recommendations.

By incorporating these treatment options and strategies into your sleep improvement journey, you create a customized roadmap toward achieving restful and rejuvenating nights. The combination of behavioral, lifestyle, and, when necessary, medical approaches contributes to a comprehensive and sustainable approach to better sleep and overall well-being.

Chapter 9

Special Considerations for Different Age Groups

Sleep Needs for Children

Understanding Children's Sleep Patterns:

Infants (0-12 months): Newborns typically sleep 14-17 hours a day, with sleep cycles lasting about 50-60 minutes. As they grow, naps become more structured.

Toddlers (1-2 years): Total sleep decreases to around 11-14 hours. Establishing a consistent bedtime routine is crucial for promoting healthy sleep habits.

Preschoolers (3-5 years): Sleep needs to stabilize at 10-13 hours. Daytime naps may reduce, emphasizing the importance of nighttime sleep.

Nightmares and Night Terrors: These may occur, requiring a comforting and reassuring bedtime routine.

Bedtime Resistance: Establishing consistent sleep routines and creating a calming environment can alleviate resistance.

Screen Time Impact: Limiting screen exposure before bedtime is essential, as it can interfere with the natural sleep-wake cycle.

Sleep Challenges in Adolescents and Young Adults

Adolescent Sleep Patterns:

Changing Sleep Patterns: Puberty triggers a shift in circadian rhythm, leading to a preference for later bedtimes and wake times.

Ideal Sleep Duration: Adolescents still need 8-10 hours of sleep, but academic and social demands may result in insufficient sleep.

Common Sleep Challenges:

Delayed Sleep Phase Syndrome (DSPS): A natural shift in circadian rhythm leads to difficulty falling asleep earlier in the evening.

Sleep Deprivation: Academic pressures, extracurricular activities, and social demands can contribute to inadequate sleep duration.

Technology Use: Excessive screen time, especially before bedtime, can disrupt sleep patterns.

Sleep in the Elderly: Addressing Changes and Challenges

Aging and Sleep:

Changes in Sleep Architecture: Older adults may experience changes in sleep architecture, including lighter sleep and more frequent awakenings.

Shifts in Circadian Rhythms: The elderly often experience a shift in circadian rhythms, leading to early morning awakening and a preference for earlier bedtimes.

Common Sleep Challenges:

Insomnia: Difficulty falling asleep or staying asleep is common among the elderly.

Sleep Apnea: Prevalence increases with age, requiring attention to symptoms such as snoring and daytime sleepiness.

Medication Impact: Some medications may interfere with sleep, emphasizing the need for regular medication reviews.

Real-World Insights

Balancing the sleep needs of my children required adapting routines as they grew. In adolescence, the challenge shifted to fostering healthy sleep habits amid academic pressures. As my parents aged, addressing their changing sleep patterns became an essential aspect of their overall well-being.

Call-to-Action

1. Establish Healthy Sleep Habits Early: For children, prioritize consistent bedtime routines and limit screen time before sleep.

2. Encourage Time Management: Adolescents should be supported in managing academic and social demands to ensure adequate sleep.

3. Regular Check-ins for the Elderly: Regularly assess sleep patterns in the elderly, address any emerging sleep challenges, and consult healthcare professionals when needed.

Understanding and addressing the unique sleep needs and challenges at different life stages is essential for cultivating a lifelong foundation of healthy sleep habits. By tailoring strategies to the specific needs of children, adolescents, and the elderly, individuals can navigate the evolving landscape of sleep with informed and proactive approaches.

Chapter 10

Troubleshooting Sleep Issues

Identifying and Overcoming Sleep Roadblocks

1. Common Sleep Roadblocks:

Stress and Anxiety: Persistent worries and stress can create mental roadblocks, hindering the ability to relax and fall asleep.

Irregular Sleep Schedule: Inconsistent bedtimes and wake times disrupt the body's internal clock, contributing to sleep difficulties.

Unhealthy Lifestyle Habits: Poor diet, lack of physical activity, and excessive caffeine or alcohol intake can negatively impact sleep.

2. *Overcoming Sleep Roadblocks:*

Stress Management: Incorporate stress-reducing practices such as mindfulness, deep breathing, or journaling into your daily routine.

Establish a Consistent Sleep Schedule: Prioritize regular bedtimes and wake times to synchronize with your body's circadian rhythm.

Promote a Healthy Lifestyle: Adopt a balanced diet, engage in regular physical activity, and limit the intake of stimulants close to bedtime.

Seeking Professional Help

1. When to Consider Professional Help:

Persistent Sleep Issues: If sleep problems persist despite implementing lifestyle changes and self-help strategies.

Impact on Daily Functioning: When sleep difficulties significantly affect daily activities, mood, and overall well-being.

Symptoms of Sleep Disorders: Presence of symptoms such as loud snoring, pauses in breathing, or restless legs that may indicate underlying sleep disorders.

2. Professional Assessment and Diagnosis:

Consult a Healthcare Provider: Begin by discussing sleep concerns with a primary care physician or a sleep specialist.

Sleep Studies: In cases of suspected sleep disorders, a healthcare provider may recommend a sleep study (polysomnography) to monitor sleep patterns and diagnose specific issues.

Mental Health Professionals: If stress, anxiety, or mental health concerns contribute to sleep problems, consulting a mental health professional can provide additional support.

3. Treatment and Intervention:

Medications: In some cases, medications may be prescribed to address specific sleep disorders or symptoms. These should be used under the guidance of a healthcare professional.

Therapeutic Interventions: Cognitive Behavioral Therapy for Insomnia (CBT-I) or other therapeutic approaches may be recommended to address underlying psychological factors contributing to sleep difficulties.

Lifestyle Modifications: Professionals can provide tailored advice on lifestyle changes to promote better sleep hygiene.

Real-World Insights

Navigating persistent sleep issues led me to seek professional help. The guidance of a healthcare provider and the insights from a sleep study were instrumental in understanding and addressing the root causes of my sleep challenges.

Call-to-Action

1. **Self-Assessment:** Reflect on the persistence and impact of your sleep issues. If sleep difficulties significantly affect your daily life, it may be time to seek professional help.

2. **Open Communication:** Discuss your sleep concerns openly with a primary care physician or sleep specialist. Be prepared to share details about sleep patterns, lifestyle, and any observed symptoms.

3. **Follow Professional Advice:** If professional intervention is recommended, follow through with suggested treatments, medications, or lifestyle changes. Regular follow-ups ensure ongoing support and adjustments as needed.

By proactively addressing sleep roadblocks and seeking professional help when necessary, individuals can reclaim restful nights and foster long-term sleep health. This chapter serves as a guide for troubleshooting sleep issues, offering insights and practical steps to navigate the path to better sleep with the support of healthcare professionals.

Conclusion

As we reach the final chapter of "The Art of Good Zzz's," it's clear that our journey through the landscape of sleep has been both enlightening and transformative. From understanding the intricacies of insomnia to unraveling the science of circadian rhythms, we've explored the diverse factors that influence our nightly repose.

Through the lens of different age groups, we've recognized the unique sleep needs of children, navigated the challenges faced by adolescents and young adults, and addressed the changes and considerations for the elderly. Each stage of life brings its own set of nuances, and empowering ourselves with knowledge allows us to adapt and foster healthy sleep habits across the lifespan.

We've troubleshooted common sleep roadblocks, identifying and overcoming challenges that may impede the journey to restful nights. Whether it's managing stress, establishing a consistent sleep schedule, or adopting a holistic lifestyle, the tools provided are stepping stones toward a more rejuvenating sleep experience.

The call-to-action resonates as an invitation to take charge of our sleep health, recognizing when to implement self-help strategies, and when to seek professional guidance. Understanding that professional help is not a sign of defeat but a proactive step toward a solution underscores the importance of prioritizing our well-being.

In the realm of sleep, we've embraced the power of mindfulness, the science behind relaxation, and the delicate dance between nutrition and rest. The holistic approach advocated in this book reflects the interconnectedness of our physical, mental, and emotional well-being with the quality of our sleep.

As you close this book, may the insights gained become the seeds of transformation in your nightly routines. Let the art of good Zzz's be your guide to a more profound understanding of sleep, an appreciation for its nuances, and the empowerment to shape your own journey toward restful and rejuvenating nights.

Remember, sleep is not merely a biological necessity; it's a fundamental aspect of a vibrant and fulfilling life. Here's to the artistry of good Zzz's and the promise of countless nights filled with the tranquility and rejuvenation that we all deserve. Sleep well, live well, and embrace the art of cultivating restorative nights for a brighter, healthier tomorrow.